ZONE 13

The Great Brain

DAVID ORME

The Great Brain
by David Orme
Illustrated by Jorge Mongiovi and Ulises Carpintero
Cover photograph: © Vladislav Ociacia

Published by Ransom Publishing Ltd.
Radley House, 8 St. Cross Road, Winchester, Hampshire, SO23 9HX, UK
www.ransom.co.uk

ISBN   978 184167 460 5
First published in 2011
Copyright © 2011 Ransom Publishing Ltd.
Illustrations copyright © 2011 Jorge Mongiovi and Ulises Carpintero

Originally published in 1998 by Stanley Thornes Publishers Ltd.

CONTENTS

4

THE INTELLIGENT ROBOT

Dr Carter was in her laboratory. Three people were with her. They came from a big company that made electrical goods. Dr Carter was showing them her new idea for an intelligent robot. It could do many of the jobs that people do now.

'What is so different about this robot?' asked Mr Yung. He was the head of Yung Products.

'It can learn!' said Dr Carter. 'It has a brain that can grow in size. When its brain is full, it grows special memory chips.'

'How does that work?' asked Mr Yung.

'It's a secret!' said Dr Carter. 'But I can tell you this. We've found a way to make special crystals grow. They become memory chips.'

The robot was just a box on wheels. It had two arms with special hands. The hands could pick things up and move them. It was called the Experimental Learning Machine. Dr Carter called it LEN. The word LEN was painted on the side.

'It is controlled by voice,' said Dr Carter. 'Watch.'

She spoke to the robot.

'LEN, sweep the floor.'

The machine rolled over to a cupboard. It opened it. It took out a brush. It started to sweep the floor.

The important people from Yung electronics laughed.

'What else can it do?' asked Mr Yung.

'There is no limit,' said Dr Carter. 'It can learn anything!'

NOT FOR THE PUBLIC TO KNOW
TOP SECRET
ZONE 13 FILES ONLY

DANGER - IEN AT WORK!

Mike Smith helped Dr Carter in the laboratory. The worst job was cleaning up at the end of the day. Dr Carter always left it in a terrible mess!

Dr Carter had gone home early. She was pleased. Mr Yung liked the new learning robot. She hoped there might be a big deal coming up – worth millions!

Mike looked round at the mess. He sighed. He hated hard work!

Suddenly he had an idea. LEN was in the corner of the room. He went over and switched it on.

'LEN, sweep the floor,' said Mike. 'Then tidy up the bench. Put everything away in the right place.'

LEN started work. Mike was pleased. Great! No work for him!

He sat down at a computer and switched it
on. He ran his favourite game – Formula 1
racing!

At last the game was over. Mike switched
off the machine. He turned round. LEN was
right behind him. The robot had a special eye.
The eye was watching the computer.

'Right', said Mike. 'Go back into your corner.'

LEN moved into the corner. Mike went out of the laboratory. He locked the door behind him.

Inside the laboratory, LEN started to move. Mike had forgotten to turn it off.

The robot moved to the computer and switched it on.

LEN loaded up the racing game and started to play. The robot was better at it than Mike. It soon got bored. It started to press other keys, to see what the computer could do.

THE NEXT DAY

Dr Carter arrived at work early the next day. She found the laboratory in a mess.

'Mike!' she said. 'I thought I told you to tidy up yesterday.'

Mike looked at the laboratory. There were things everywhere. He was about to say that he *had* tidied up. Then he remembered that LEN had done it. He wasn't supposed to touch LEN. He decided not to say anything.

'I'll do it now,' he said.

Mike started to tidy up. He looked at the equipment. It wasn't the same things that had been left out yesterday. What had happened?

'Oh no!' thought Mike. 'I bet I didn't turn LEN off last night!'

He looked at LEN. The robot was switched off.

'Perhaps I did switch it off after all,' thought Mike. 'I wonder who made this mess?'

He started tidying up. Suddenly he felt something grab his leg.

'Leave that alone!' said a voice.

Mike looked down. LEN had left its corner. Its metal hand was holding Mike's leg. The robot had learnt to switch itself on and off!

'Let go!' said Mike. 'That hurts!'

LEN's other arm came up. It grabbed Mike's jacket. The robot pushed Mike towards the door. It let go of Mike's leg and opened the

door. Then it pushed Mike out. The door slammed.

'Help!' yelled Mike. 'The robot's gone mad!'

Dr Carter came running up. Mike told her what had happened.

'You fool, Mike! You know that LEN is only an experiment. Anything could happen!'

They tried to open the door. LEN had locked it.

'Quick!' said Dr Carter. 'Let's check the security camera.'

There was a camera in the laboratory. They could see what was going on inside, on a monitor screen.

They soon worked out what LEN was up to.

He was building another robot out of spare parts.

THE SECOND ROBOT

Dr Carter called security. They had to get into that laboratory.

The security man arrived with an axe. He chopped a hole in the door. A metal arm came through the hole and grabbed the axe. The security guard got away just in time.

Dr Carter and Mike went back to the TV screen.

LEN looked different now. Dr Carter guessed what was happening.

'It's the brain! It's growing!' she said.

The brain section of the robot was twice as big now. The robot was learning at an amazing rate.

The computer was running. The new robot that LEN had made was watching the screen.

'LEN is teaching it!' said Dr Carter.

Then she noticed something. This robot didn't have LEN painted on the side. This one was called LIL.

Mike had to laugh. 'LEN has made himself a girlfriend!' he said.

Dr Carter didn't think it was funny at all. It was very serious. She decided to call in other robot scientists to help her.

'They must be stopped!' she said. 'Their brains will just keep on growing!'

One of the other scientists looked worried.

'That robot can grow, and learn, and even make other robots like itself. It isn't a machine any longer. It's alive!'

The monitor screen stopped working. LEN and LIL didn't like being watched, and they had switched off the camera. Now no one knew what was happening.

At last, there was a crash. LEN and LIL had broken out. They were setting off down the road for the local town!

'They must be stopped!' said Dr Carter. 'They can't move very fast!'

She was wrong. The robots were moving at amazing speed!

Mike groaned.

'Oh no!' he said. 'It was that racing car game. They have learnt to go fast!'

THE ROBOTS HIT TOWN

The robots were causing trouble in town. They were stealing all sorts of things. Dr Carter guessed that they were looking for stuff to build more robots with. It was dangerous to get in their way. Many people were hurt trying to stop them.

Later in the day, the robots got back to the laboratory. Dr Carter and the others could hear them hard at work.

The next morning there was silence from the laboratory. At last the door opened. The robot called LIL came out.

'Where is Dr Carter?' asked LIL.

Dr Carter went into the laboratory. LEN was in the middle of the room.

'LEN does not work now,' said LIL. 'You made him. What is wrong?'

Dr Carter looked at LEN. His brain was huge now but something was wrong. It was starting to crumble away.

Dr Carter remembered what the other scientist had said.

'It isn't a machine any longer. It's alive!'

Living things weren't the same as machines. They could die.

'His brain has grown too fast', said Dr Carter. 'I'm afraid that LEN is dead.'

'Will that happen to me too?' asked LIL.

'Yes,' said Dr Carter. 'I'm afraid so.'

LIL moved over to the body of LEN. The new robot reached out a metal arm, and turned itself off. It was as if LIL couldn't bear to live without LEN.

Dr Carter laughed. What a silly idea! They were only machines, after all.

She sat down at the computer. A brain that could mend itself. That was what was needed. She would soon work out how to do that.

Dr Carter thought about the future. The world would be full of her robots. Soon everything would be done by them.

There would be no need for people at all.

ABOUT THE AUTHOR

David Orme is an expert on strange, unexplained events. For his protection (and yours) we cannot show a photograph of him.

David created the Zone 13 files to record the cases he studied. Some of these files really do involve aliens, but many do not. Aliens are not everywhere. Just in most places.

These stories are all taken from the Zone 13 files. They will not be here for long. Read them while you can.

But don't close your eyes when you go to sleep at night. **They** will be watching you.